kids ESSENTIAL KNITS

ten hand knit
childrens designs

quail studio

quail studio

Published in 2017 by
Quail Publishing
The Old Forge
Market Square
Toddington
Bedfordshire, LU5 6BP
UK

ISBN: 978-0-9935908-1-8

Conceived, designed and produced by

q u a i l s t u d i o

Art Editor: Georgina Brant
Graphic Design: Quail Studio
Technical Editor: Emma Osmond
Pattern Checking: Jill Gray
Photography: Tom Leighton
(photosbytomtom.com)
Creative Director: Darren Brant
Yarn Support: Rowan Yarns
Designer: Quail Studio
Models: Indiana & Austin
Location: The Royal National Rose Society -
Gardens of the Rose

Printed in the UK

British Library Cataloguing in Publication Data
A catalogue record for this book is available from the British Library

@quail_studio

CONTENTS

iNTRODUCTiON

The third in the series of ESSENTIAL knits from quail studio comes
the Kids collection. Designed to be a wearable all round collection for
kids. Giving a 'preppy' 'stylish' look to kids hand knitwear.

The quail studio team have taken simple shapes, paired with a
vibrant colour palette to bring to life the exquisite yarn from Rowan.

Featuring a core collection of hand knit sweaters, cardigans and
acessories that will see your children through the chilly spring months.
Designed to last, the garments will become a core staple in your
childrens wardrobe year upon year.

We just know you will not be disappointed!

quail studio team
xOxO

JESSE
rowan big wool

JAMIE
rowan handknit cotton

CHARLIE
rowan big wool

TAYLOR
rowan handknit cotton

INDIANA &
AUSTIN
rowan summerlite
DK

HENRY & POPPY
rowan summerlite 4ply

EDWARD & ALICE
rowan summerlite 4ply & cotton glace

jesse

chunky jacket

SIZE: To fit age 4-6(6-8, 8-10) years

YARN USAGE:
Rowan Big Wool
A – shown in Prize - 064 and
Smokey – 007, 4(4, 5) x 100g

B – shown in Blue Velvet - 026 and
Reseda – 069, 1(1, 1) x 100g

NEEDLES:
8mm (US 11) and 10mm (US 15) needles

EXTRAS:
Stitch Holder
6 x Buttons

TENSION:
10sts and 12rows = 10cms
measured over st st using
10mm needles.

BACK:
Using 8mm needles and Yarn A, cast on
34(38, 42)sts.
Row 1: (RS) (K2, P2) to last 2 sts, K2.
Row 2: (P2, K2) to last 2 sts, P2.
Change to Yarn B.
Row 3: As row 1.
Row 4: As row 2.
Change to Yarn A.
Row 5: As row 1.
Row 6: As row 2.

Change to Yarn B and 10mm needles,
starting with a K row work in st st for
2 rows.

Break off yarn B.

Change to Yarn A, cont in st st until back
meas 26.5(30.5, 34.5)cm, ending with a
WS row.

Shape armholes
Cast off 2sts at beg of next 2 rows.
30[34, 38]sts.
Dec 1 st at each end of next row.
28[32, 36]sts.

Cont straight until armhole meas
17(17.5, 18)cm, ending with a WS row.

Shape back neck
Next Row: K6(8, 10) turn, leaving rem sts
on a stitch holder.
Work each side of neck separately.
Dec 1 st at neck edge on next row.
5[7, 9]sts.
Cast off.

With RS facing, slip centre 16sts onto
a stitch holder, rejoin Yarn A and knit
to end.

Complete to match first side,
reversing shapings.

LEFT FRONT:
Using 8mm needles and Yarn A, cast on
18(18, 22)sts.

Work in rib stripe pattern as given for
back, dec 2 sts evenly across last row for
1st and 3rd sizes. 16[18, 20]sts.

Change to Yarn B and 10mm needles,
starting with a K row work in st st for
2 rows.

Break off Yarn B.

Change to Yarn A, cont in st st until left
front meas 26.5(30.5, 34.5)cm, ending
with a WS row.

Shape armholes
Cast off 2sts at beg of next row.
14[16, 18]sts.
Next row: Purl.
Dec 1 st at armhole edge on next row.
13[15, 17]sts.

Cont straight until armhole meas 11cm,
ending with a RS row.

Shape neck
Next Row: Cast off, 6sts, work to end.
7[9, 11]sts.
Dec 1 st at neck edge on next and foll alt
row. 5[7, 9]sts.
Cont straight until work matches same
length as back, ending with a WS row.
Cast off.

RIGHT FRONT:

Work as given for Left Front reversing
all shapings.

SLEEVES:
Using 8mm needles and Yarn A,
cast on 18sts.

Work in rib stripe pattern as given
for back.

Change to Yarn B and 10mm needles,
starting with a K row work in st st for
2 rows.

Change to Yarn A, cont in st st, inc 1 st
at each end of next and every alt row to

24sts and every foll 4th row to 34(34, 36)sts.

Cont straight until sleeve meas 28.5(31, 34)cm ending with a WS row.

Shape sleeve top
Cast off 2sts at beg of next 2 rows. 30[30, 32]sts.
Dec 1 st at each end of next row. 28[28, 30]sts.
Work 1 row.
Cast off.

FINISHING:
Press as described on the information page.
Join both shoulder seams.

Button band:
BOYS
With RS facing, using 8mm needles and Yarn A, beg at cast-on edge pick up and knit 42(42, 50)sts along right front edge.

Row 1: (WS) (P2, K2) to last 2 sts, P2.
Row 2: (K2, P2) to last 2sts, K2.
Row 3: As row 1.
Cast off in rib.

GIRLS
With RS facing, using 8mm needles and Yarn A, beg at cast-off sts at neck edge pick up and knit 42(42, 50)sts along left front edge.
Row 1: (WS) (P2, K2) to last 2 sts, P2.
Row 2: (K2, P2) to last 2sts, K2.
Row 3: As row 1.
Cast off in rib.

Button hole band:
BOYS
With RS facing, using 8mm needles and Yarn A, beg at cast-off sts at neck edge pick up and knit 42(42, 50)sts along left front edge.
Row 1: (WS) (P2, K2) to last 2 sts, P2.
Row 2: (Button hole row) K2, *P2tog, yon, patt 6sts, rep from * to end.
Row 3: As row 1.
Cast off in rib.

GIRLS
With RS facing, using 8mm needles and Yarn A, beg at cast-on edge pick up and knit 42(42, 50)sts along right front edge.

Row 1: (WS) (P2, K2) to last 2 sts, P2.
Row 2: (Button hole row *Patt 6sts, yfwd, yrn, k2tog, rep from * to last 2sts, K2.
Row 3: As row 1.
Cast off in rib.

Collar:
With RS facing, 8mm needles and Yarn A, beg halfway across right front band pick up and knit 2sts from right front band, 14sts up right side of front neck, 3sts down right side of back neck , 16sts from stitch holder, 3sts up left side of back neck, 14sts down left side of front neck, 2sts across left front band, ending halfway across left front band. (54sts).

Row 1: (RS of collar, WS of work) K2, (P2, K2) to end.
Row 2: (P2, K2) to last 2sts, P2.
Rep last 2 rows 4 times more.
Work 2 rows in rib in Yarn B.
Work 1 row in rib in Yarn A.
Cast off in rib.

Sew in sleeves.
Join side and sleeve seams.
Attach buttons.

BOYS & GIRLS VERSION

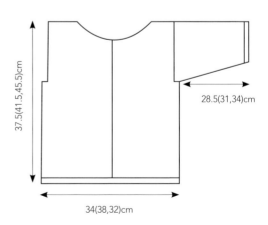

37.5(41.5,45.5)cm

28.5(31,34)cm

34(38,32)cm

ʒAMje

rugby sweater
boys/girls version

BOYS VERSION

SIZE: To fit age 4-5(5-6, 6-7, 7-8, 8-9, 9-10) years

YARN USAGE:
Rowan Handknit Cotton
A – shown in Turkish Plum 277
3(3, 3, 4, 4, 4) x 50g

B - shown in Cloud 345
4(4, 4, 5, 5, 5) x 50g

NEEDLES:
3.25mm (US 3) and 4mm (US 6) needles

EXTRAS:
Stich Holders
3 x Buttons

TENSION:
20sts and 28rows = 10cm
Measured over st st using 4mm needles

BACK:
Using 3.25mm needles and Yarn A, cast on 74(74, 78, 82, 86, 86)sts.

Row 1: (RS) (K2, P2) to last 2 sts, K2.

Row 2: (P2, K2) to last 2 sts, P2.

Rep last 2 rows twice more, dec 2 sts evenly across last row.
72[72, 76, 80, 84, 84]sts.

Narrow stripe sequence

Rows 1 - 16: B
Rows 17 & 18: A

Change to 4mm needles, starting with a K row work in st st keeping stripe pattern correct, repeat rows 1 to 18 throughout until back meas 23(26.5, 28, 30.5, 33.5, 34.5)cm, ending with a WS row.

Shape armholes
Cast off 2sts at beg of next 2 rows.
68[68, 72, 76, 80, 80]sts.
Dec 1 st at each end of next and 3 foll alt
rows. 60[60, 64, 68, 72, 72]sts. **

Cont straight until armhole meas
17(17, 17, 17.5, 18, 18)cm, ending with a
WS row.

Shape neck
Next Row: K15(15, 17, 17, 18, 18) turn,
leaving rem sts on a stitch holder.
Work each side of neck separately.
Dec 1 st at neck edge on next row.
14[14, 16, 16, 17, 17]sts.
Cast off.

With RS facing, slip centre 30(30, 30,
34, 36, 36)sts onto a stitch holder, rejoin
appropriate colour and knit to end.
Complete to match first side, reversing
shapings.

FRONT:
Work as given for back to **.
Cont straight until armhole meas 7cm,
ending with a WS row.

Divide for front opening:
Next Row: K27(27, 29, 31, 33, 33) turn,
leaving rem sts on a stitch holder.
Work each side of neck separately.
Cont straight until armhole meas 12cm,
ending with a RS row.

Shape Neck:
Next Row: Cast off 4sts, purl to end.
23[23, 25, 27, 29, 29]sts
Next Row: Knit
Next Row: P2, P2tog, purl to end.
22[22, 24, 26, 28, 28]sts.
Dec 1 st at neck edge on every row until
14(14, 16, 16, 17, 17)sts remain.
Cont straight until work matches length
of back, ending with a WS row.
Cast off.

With RS facing, rejoin appropriate colour
to remaining sts, cast off 6sts and knit to
end. 27[27, 29, 31, 33, 33]sts. Complete
to match first side, reversing shapings.

SLEEVES:
Using 3.25mm needles and Yarn A, cast
on 38(38, 38, 42, 42, 42)sts.
Row 1: (RS) (K2, P2) to last 2 sts, K2.
Row 2: (P2, K2) to last 2 sts, P2.
Rep last 2 rows twice more, dec 2 sts
evenly across last row.
36[36, 36, 40, 40, 40]sts.

Change to 4mm needles, starting with
a K row work in st st, keeping stripe
sequence correct as given for back.

Inc 1 st each end of 5th and every
following 4th row to
64(64, 64, 70, 72, 72)sts.

Cont straight until sleeve meas 27(28.5,
30, 31, 32, 34)cm, ending with a WS row.

Shape sleeve top
Cast off 2sts at beg of next 2 rows.
60[60, 60, 66, 68, 68]sts.
Dec 1 st at each end of next and 3 foll alt
rows. 52[52, 52, 58, 60, 60]sts.
Work 1 row.
Cast off.

FINISHING:
Press as described on the information page.
Join both shoulder seams.

Button hole band
With RS facing, using 3.25mm needles and Yarn A, beg at neck shaping pick up and knit 14sts down left side of opening.
Row 1: (WS) (P2, K2) to last 2 sts, P2.
Row 2: (K2, P2) to last 2 sts, K2.
Row 3: Patt 1, * patt2tog, yrn, patt 2sts, rep from * to last st, patt 1.
Row 4: As row 2.
Row 5: As row 1.
Row 6: As row 2.
Cast off in rib.

Button band
With RS facng, using 3.25mm needles and Yarn A, beg at base of opening pick up and knit 14sts up right side of opening.
Row 1: (WS) (P2, K2) to last 2 sts, P2.
Row 2: (K2, P2) to last 2 sts, K2.
Rep last 2 rows twice more.
Cast off in rib.

Collar
With RS facing, using 3.25mm needles and Yarn A, beg halfway across button band pick up and knit 3sts from button band, 13(13, 13, 15, 16, 16)sts up right side of front neck, 2sts down right side of back neck, 30(30, 30, 34, 36, 36) sts from stitch holder, 2sts up left side of back neck, 13(13, 13, 15, 16, 16)sts down left side of front neck, and 3sts from button hole band, ending halfway across button hole band.
66[66, 66, 74, 78, 78]sts
Row 1: (RS of collar, WS of work) (K2, P2) to last 2 sts, K2.
Row 2: (P2, K2) to last 2 sts, P2.
Rep last 2 rows until collar meas 10cm, ending with a WS row.
Cast off in rib.

Sew in sleeves.

Join side and sleeve seams.

Attach buttons.

GIRLS VERSION

SIZE: To fit age 4-5(5-6, 6-7, 7-8, 8-9, 9-10) years

YARN USAGE:
Rowan Handknit Cotton

A – shown in Florence 350 – 3(3, 3, 4, 4, 4) x 50g

B - shown in Bleached 263 – 4(4, 4, 5, 5, 5) x 50g

NEEDLES:
3.25mm (US 3) and 4mm (US 6) needles

EXTRAS:
Stitch Holders
3 x Buttons

TENSION: 20sts and 28rows = 10cm
Measured over st st using 4mm needles

BACK:
Using 3.25mm needles and yarn A, cast on 74(74, 78, 82, 86, 86)sts.
Row 1: (RS) (K2, P2) to last 2 sts, K2.
Row 2: (P2, K2) to last 2 sts, P2.
Rep last 2 rows twice more, dec 2 sts evenly across last row.
72[72, 76, 80, 84, 84]sts.

Narrow stripe sequence
Rows 1 - 16: B
Rows 17 & 18: A

Change to 4mm needles, starting with a K row work in st st keeping stripe pattern correct, repeat rows 1 to 18 throughout until back meas 23(26.5, 28, 30.5, 33.5, 34.5)cm, ending with a WS row.

Shape armholes
Cast off 2sts at beg of next 2 rows.
68[68, 72, 76, 80, 80]sts.

Dec 1 st at each end of next and 3 foll alt rows. 60[60, 64, 68, 72, 72]sts. **

Cont straight until armhole meas 17(17, 17, 17.5, 18, 18)cm, ending with a WS row.

Shape neck
Next Row: K15(15, 17, 17, 18, 18) turn, leaving rem sts on a stitch holder.

Work each side of neck separately.

Dec 1 st at neck edge on next row. 14[14, 16, 16, 17, 17]sts.

Cast off.

With RS facing, slip centre 30(30, 30, 34, 36, 36)sts onto a stitch holder, rejoin appropriate colour and knit to end. Complete to match first side, reversing shapings.

FRONT:
Work as given for back to **.

Cont straight until armhole meas 7cm, ending with a WS row.

Divide for front opening:
Next Row: K27(27, 29, 31, 33, 33) turn, leaving rem sts on a stitch holder.

Work each side of neck separately.

Cont straight until armhole meas 12cm, ending with a RS row.

Shape Neck:
Next Row: Cast off 4sts, purl to end. 23[23, 25, 27, 29, 29]sts
Next Row: Knit
Next Row: P2, P2tog, purl to end. 22[22, 24, 26, 28, 28]sts.
Dec 1 st at neck edge on every row until 14(14, 16, 16, 17, 17)sts remain.
Cont straight until work matches length of back, ending with a WS row.

Cast off.

With RS facing, rejoin appropriate colour to remaining sts, cast off 6sts and knit to end. 27[27, 29, 31, 33, 33]sts. Complete to match first side, reversing shapings.

SLEEVES:
Using 3.25mm needles and Yarn A, cast on 38(38, 38, 42, 42, 42)sts.
Row 1: (RS) (K2, P2) to last 2 sts, K2.

Row 2: (P2, K2) to last 2 sts, P2.
Rep last 2 rows twice more, dec 2 sts evenly across last row.
36[36, 36, 40, 40, 40]sts.

Change to 4mm needles, starting with a K row work in st st, keeping stripe sequence correct as given for back.

Inc 1 st each end of 5th and every foll 4th row to 64(64, 64, 70, 72, 72)sts.

Cont straight until sleeve meas 27(28.5, 30, 31, 32, 34)cm, ending with a WS row.

Shape sleeve top
Cast off 2sts at beg of next 2 rows.
60[60, 60, 66, 68, 68]sts.
Dec 1 st at each end of next and 3 foll alt rows. 52[52, 52, 58, 60, 60]sts.
Work 1 row.
Cast off.

FINISHING:
Press as described on the information page.
Join both shoulder seams.

Button hole band
With RS facing, using 3.25mm needles and Yarn A, beg at base of opening pick up and knit 14sts up right side of opening.
Row 1: (WS) (P2, K2) to last 2 sts, P2.
Row 2: (K2, P2) to last 2 sts, K2.
Row 3: Patt 2, * patt2tog, yrn, patt 2sts, rep from * to end.
Row 4: As row 2.
Row 5: As row 1.
Row 6: As row 2.
Cast off in rib.

Button band
With RS facing, using 3.25mm needles and Yarn A, beg at neck shaping pick up and knit 14sts down left side of opening.
Row 1: (WS) (P2, K2) to last 2 sts, P2.
Row 2: (K2, P2) to last 2 sts, K2.
Rep last 2 rows twice more.
Cast off in rib.

Collar
With RS facing, using 3.25mm needles
and Yarn A, beg halfway across button
band pick up and knit 3sts from button
band, 13(13, 13, 15, 16, 16)sts up right
side of front neck, 2sts down right side
of back neck, 30(30, 30, 34, 36, 36)
sts from stitch holder, 2sts up left side
of back neck, 13(13, 13, 15, 16, 16)sts
down left side of front neck, and 3sts
from button hole band, ending halfway
across button hole band.
66[66, 66, 74, 78, 78]sts
Row 1: (RS of collar, WS of work) (K2, P2)
to last 2 sts, K2.
Row 2: (P2, K2) to last 2 sts, P2.
Rep last 2 rows until collar meas 10cm,
ending with a WS row.
Cast off in rib.

Sew in sleeves.

Join side and sleeve seams.

Attach buttons.

BOYS & GIRLS VERSION

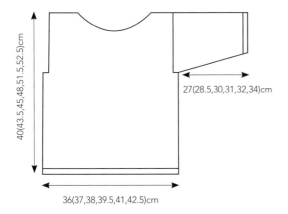

40(43.5,45,48,51.5,52.5)cm

27(28.5,30,31,32,34)cm

36(37,38,39.5,41,42.5)cm

CHARLie
hat & snood

CHARLIE HAT
SIZE: To fit age 4-7(7-10) years

YARN USAGE: Rowan Big Wool
Girls Version – Pantomime 079 -
2 x 100g

Boys Version – Blue Velvet 026 –
2 x 100g

(If you choose not to add the Pom Pom
you will need 1 x 100g ball)

NEEDLES: 10mm (US 15) needles

EXTRAS: Pom Pom maker (optional)

TENSION: 9sts and 13rows = 10cm
measured over patt using
10mm (US15) needles

Using 10mm needles cast on 46(54)sts.
Row 1: (RS) * K1, P1, rep from * to end.
Rep row 1 until hat measures 3cm,
ending with a WS row.

Row 1: P2 * K1, P3, rep from * to end.
Row 2: * K3, P1, rep from * to last 2sts,
K2.

These 2 rows from patt

Cont in patt until hat meas 16cm,
ending with a WS row.

Shape crown
Next Row: P2tog * K1, P2tog, P1, rep
from * to end. 34[40]sts.
Next Row: * K2, P1, rep from * to last st,
K1.
Next Row: P1 *K1, P2tog, rep from * to
end. 23[27]sts
Next Row: * K1, P1, rep from * to end.
Next Row: * K2tog rep from * to end.
12[14]sts.

Next Row: * P2tog rep from * to end.
6[7]sts.
Break yarn and thread through rem
6[7]sts. Pull up tight and fasten
off securely.

FINISHING:
Press as described on the
information page.

Join back seam, reversing seam for turn
back if desired. Make pom pom approx
8cm in circumference or desired size,
attach securely to top of hat.

CHARLIE SNOOD
SIZES: One size

YARN USAGE: Rowan Big Wool

Girls Version – Shown in Pantomime 079
- 1 x 100g

Boys Version – Shown in Blue Velvet 026
– 1 x 100g

NEEDLES: 10mm (US 15) needles

TENSION: 9sts and 13rows = 10cm
measured over patt using 10mm (US15)
needles

Approx finished measurements - 65cm
circumference x 15cm height

Using 10mm needles, cast on 59sts.
Row 1: P3, * K1, P3, rep from *
to end.
Row 2: * K3, P1, rep from * to last 3sts,
K3.
Rep last 2 rows 18 times more.
Cast off in pattern.

FINISHING:
Press as described on the
information page.
Join row-ends to form a loop.

TAYLOR

rugby sweater
boys/girls version

BOYS VERSION
SIZE: To fit age 4-5(5-6, 6-7, 7-8, 8-9,
9-10) years

YARN USAGE:
Rowan Handknit Cotton
A – shown in Gooseberry 219
3(3, 3, 4, 4, 4) x 50g

B - shown in Turkish Plum 277
4(4, 4, 5, 5, 5) x 50g

NEEDLES:
3.25mm (US 3) and 4mm (US 6) needles

EXTRAS:
Stitch Holder
3 x Buttons

TENSION:
20sts and 28rows = 10cm
measured over st st using 4mm needles

BACK:
Using 3.25mm needles and Yarn A, cast
on 74(74, 78, 82, 86, 86)sts.
Row 1: (RS) (K2, P2) to last 2 sts, K2.
Row 2: (P2, K2) to last 2 sts, P2.
Rep last 2 rows twice more, dec 2 sts
evenly across last row.
72[72, 76, 80, 84, 84]sts.

Bold stripe sequence
Rows 1 - 10: A
Rows 11- 27: B
Rows 28- 44: A

Change to 4mm needles, starting with a
K row and keeping stripe pattern correct
work 44 rows in st st, repeating rows 11
to 44 throughout cont in st st until back
meas 23(26.5, 28, 30.5, 33.5, 34.5)cm,
ending with a WS row.

Shape armholes
Cast off 2sts at beg of next 2 rows.
68[68, 72, 76, 80, 80]sts.
Dec 1 st at each end of next and 3 foll alt
rows. 60[60, 64, 68, 72, 72]sts. **

Cont straight until armhole meas
17(17, 17, 17.5, 18, 18)cm, ending with a
WS row.

Shape neck
Next Row: K15(15, 17, 17, 18, 18) turn,
leaving rem sts on a stitch holder.
Work each side of neck separately.
Dec 1 st at neck edge on next row.
14[14, 16, 16, 17, 17]sts.
Cast off.

With RS facing, slip centre 30(30, 30,
34, 36, 36)sts onto a stitch holder, rejoin
appropriate colour and knit to end.
Complete to match first side, reversing
shapings.

FRONT:
Work as given for back to **.
Cont straight until armhole meas 7cm,
ending with a WS row.

Divide for front opening:
Next Row: K27(27, 29, 31, 33, 33) turn,
leaving rem sts on a stitch holder.
Work each side of neck separately.
Cont straight until armhole meas 12cm,
ending with a RS row.

Shape Neck:
Next Row: Cast off 4sts, purl to end.
23[23, 25, 27, 29, 29]sts
Next Row: Knit
Next Row: P2, P2tog, purl to end.
22[22, 24, 26, 28, 28]sts.
Dec 1 st at neck edge on every row until
14(14, 16, 16, 17, 17)sts remain.
Cont straight until work matches length
of back, ending with a WS row.
Cast off.

With RS facing, rejoin appropriate colour
to remaining sts, cast off 6sts and knit to
end. 27[27, 29, 31, 33, 33]sts. Complete
to match first side, reversing shapings.

SLEEVES:
Using 3.25mm needles and Yarn A, cast
on 38(38, 38, 42, 42, 42)sts.
Row 1: (RS) (K2, P2) to last 2 sts, K2.
Row 2: (P2, K2) to last 2 sts, P2.
Rep last 2 rows twice more, dec 2 sts
evenly across last row.
36[36, 36, 40, 40, 40]sts.

Change to 4mm needles, starting with
a K row work in st st, keeping stripe
sequence correct as given for back.

Inc 1 st at each end of 5th and every foll
4th row to 64(64, 64, 70, 72, 72)sts.

Cont straight until sleeve meas
27(28.5, 30, 31, 32, 34)cm, ending with a
WS row.

Shape sleeve top
Cast off 2sts at beg of next 2 rows.
60[60, 60, 66, 68, 68]sts.
Dec 1 st at each end of next and 3 foll alt
rows. 52[52, 52, 58, 60, 60]sts.
Work 1 row.
Cast off.

FINISHING:
Press as described on the information page.
Join both shoulder seams.

Button hole band
With RS facing, using 3.25mm needles and Yarn B, beg at neck shaping pick up and knit 14sts down left side of opening.
Row 1: (WS) (P2, K2) to last 2 sts, P2.
Row 2: (K2, P2) to last 2 sts, K2.
Row 3: Patt 1, * patt2tog, yrn, patt 2sts, rep from * to last st, patt 1.
Row 4: As row 2.
Row 5: As row 1.
Row 6: As row 2.
Cast off in rib.

Button band
With RS facing, using 3.25mm needles and Yarn B, beg at base of opening pick up and knit 14sts up right side of opening.
Row 1: (WS) (P2, K2) to last 2 sts, P2.
Row 2: (K2, P2) to last 2 sts, K2.
Rep last 2 rows twice more.
Cast off in rib.

Collar
With RS facing, using 3.25mm needles and Yarn B, beg halfway across button band pick up and knit 3sts from button band, 13(13, 13, 15, 16, 16)sts up right side of front neck, 2sts down right side of back neck, 30(30, 30, 34, 36, 36) sts from stitch holder, 2sts up left side of back neck, 13(13, 13, 15, 16, 16)sts down left side of front neck, and 3sts from button hole band, ending halfway across button hole band.
66[66, 66, 74, 78, 78]sts
Row 1: (RS of collar, WS of work) (K2, P2) to last 2 sts, K2.
Row 2: (P2, K2) to last 2 sts, P2.
Rep last 2 rows until collar meas 10cm, ending with a WS row.
Cast off in rib.

Sew in sleeves.

Join side and sleeve seams.

Attach buttons.

GIRLS VERSION
SIZE: To fit age 4-5(5-6, 6-7, 7-8, 8-9, 9-10) years

YARN USAGE:
Rowan Handknit Cotton
A – shown in Sugar 303
3(3, 3, 4, 4, 4) x 50g

B – shown in Celery 309
4(4, 4, 5, 5, 5) x 50g

NEEDLES:
3.25mm (US 3) and 4mm (US 6) needles

EXTRAS:
Stitch Holder
3 x Buttons

TENSION:
20sts and 28 rows = 10cm measured over st st using 4mm needles

BACK:
Using 3.25mm needles and Yarn A, cast on 74(74, 78, 82, 86, 86)sts.
Row 1: (RS) (K2, P2) to last 2 sts, K2.
Row 2: (P2, K2) to last 2 sts, P2.
Rep last 2 rows twice more, dec 2 sts evenly across last row.
72[72, 76, 80, 84, 84]sts.

Bold stripe sequence
Rows 1 - 10: A
Rows 11- 27: B
Rows 28- 44: A

Change to 4mm needles, starting with a K row and keeping stripe pattern correct work 44 rows in st st, repeating rows 11 to 44 throughout cont in st st until back meas 23(26.5, 28, 30.5, 33.5, 34.5)cm, ending with a WS row.

Shape armholes
Cast off 2sts at beg of next 2 rows.
68[68, 72, 76, 80, 80]sts.
Dec 1 st at each end of next and 3 foll alt rows. 60[60, 64, 68, 72, 72]sts. **

Cont straight until armhole meas 17(17, 17, 17.5, 18, 18)cm, ending with a WS row.

Shape neck
Next Row: K15(15, 17, 17, 18, 18) turn, leaving rem sts on a stitch holder.

Work each side of neck separately.

Dec 1 st at neck edge on next row. 14[14, 16, 16, 17, 17]sts.

Cast off.

With RS facing, slip centre 30(30, 30, 34, 36, 36)sts onto a stitch holder, rejoin appropriate colour and knit to end. Complete to match first side, reversing shapings.

FRONT:
Work as given for back to **.
Cont straight until armhole meas 7cm, ending with a WS row.

Divide for front opening:
Next Row: K27(27, 29, 31, 33, 33) turn, leaving rem sts on a stitch holder.

Work each side of neck separately.

Cont straight until armhole meas 12cm, ending with a RS row.

Shape Neck:
Next Row: Cast off 4sts, purl to end.
23[23, 25, 27, 29, 29]sts
Next Row: Knit
Next Row: P2, P2tog, purl to end.
22[22, 24, 26, 28, 28]sts.
Dec 1 st at neck edge on every row until 14(14, 16, 16, 17, 17)sts remain.
Cont straight until work matches length of back, ending with a WS row.
Cast off.

With RS facing, rejoin appropriate colour to remaining sts, cast off 6sts and knit to end. 27[27, 29, 31, 33, 33]sts. Complete to match first side, reversing shapings.

SLEEVES:
Using 3.25mm needles and Yarn A, cast on 38(38, 38, 42, 42, 42)sts.
Row 1: (RS) (K2, P2) to last 2 sts, K2.

Row 2: (P2, K2) to last 2 sts, P2.
Rep last 2 rows twice more, dec 2 sts evenly across last row.
36[36, 36, 40, 40, 40]sts.

Change to 4mm needles, staring with a K row work in st st, keeping stripe sequence correct as given for back.

Inc 1 st each end of 5th and every foll 4th row to 64(64, 64, 70, 72, 72)sts.

Cont straight until sleeve meas 27(28.5, 30, 31, 32, 34)cm, ending with a WS row.

Shape sleeve top
Cast off 2sts at beg of next 2 rows.
60[60, 60, 66, 68, 68]sts.
Dec 1 st at each end of next and 3 foll alt rows. 52[52, 52, 58, 60, 60]sts.
Work 1 row.
Cast off.

FINISHING:
Press as described on the information page.
Join both shoulder seams.
Button hole band

With RS facing, using 3.25mm needles and Yarn A, beg at base of opening pick up and knit 14sts up right side of opening.
Row 1: (WS) (P2, K2) to last 2 sts, P2.
Row 2: (K2, P2) to last 2 sts, K2.
Row 3: Patt 2, * patt2tog, yrn, patt 2sts, rep from * to end.
Row 4: As row 2.
Row 5: As row 1.
Row 6: As row 2.
Cast off in rib.

Button band
With RS facing, using 3.25mm needles and Yarn A, beg at neck shaping pick up and knit 14sts down left side of opening.
Row 1 (WS): (P2, K2) to last 2 sts, P2.
Row 2: (K2, P2) to last 2 sts, K2.
Rep last 2 rows twice more.
Cast off in rib.

Collar
With RS facing, using 3.25mm needles and Yarn A, beg halfway across button band pick up and knit 3sts from button band, 13(13, 13, 15, 16, 16)sts up right side of front neck, 2sts down right side of back neck, 30(30, 30, 34, 36, 36) sts from stitch holder, 2sts up left side of back neck, 13(13, 13, 15, 16, 16)sts down left side of front neck, and 3sts from button hole band, ending halfway across button hole band.
66[66, 66, 74, 78, 78]sts

Row 1: (RS of collar, WS of work) (K2, P2) to last 2 sts, K2.
Row 2: (P2, K2) to last 2 sts, P2.
Rep last 2 rows until collar meas 10cm, ending with a WS row.
Cast off in rib.

Sew in sleeves.

Join side and sleeve seams.

Attach buttons.

BOYS AND GIRLS VERSION

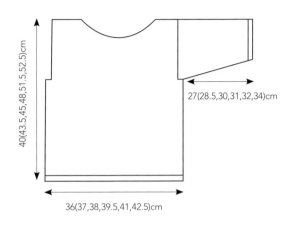

40(43.5,45,48,51.5,52.5)cm

27(28.5,30,31,32,34)cm

36(37,38,39.5,41,42.5)cm

iNdiANA

cardigan

SIZE: To fit age 4-5(5-6, 6-7, 7-8, 8-9, 9-10) years

Yarn Usage:
Rowan Summerlite DK shown in Pear 463 – 5(5, 6, 6, 6, 6) x 50g

Needle:
3.25mm (US 3) and 4mm (US 6) needles

EXTRAS:
Stitch Holder
7 x Buttons

Tension:
22sts and 30rows = 10cm
Measured over st st using 4mm needles

BACK:
Using 3.25mm needles, cast on 81(85, 85, 89, 93, 97)sts.
Row 1: (RS) P1, (K3, P1) to end.
Row 2: (K1, P3) to last st, K1.

These 2 rows form rib.
Rep last 2 rows until back meas 6cm, dec 1 st in centre of last row, ending with a WS row.
80[84, 84, 88, 92, 96]sts.

Change to 4mm needles, starting with a K row work in st st until back meas 23(26.5, 28, 30.5, 33.5, 34.5)cm, ending with a WS row.

Shape armholes
Cast off 3sts at beg of next 2 rows.
74[78, 78, 82, 86, 90]sts.
Dec 1 st at each end of next and 3 foll alt rows. 66[70, 70, 74, 78, 82]sts.

Cont straight until armhole meas 17(17, 17, 17.5, 18, 18)cm, ending with a WS row.

Shape back neck
Next Row: K17(19, 19, 19, 19, 21) turn,
leaving rem sts on a stitch holder.
Work each side of neck separately.
Dec 1 st at neck edge on next row.
16[18, 18, 18, 18, 20]sts.
Cast off.

With RS facing, slip centre 32(32, 32, 36,
40, 40)sts onto a stitch holder, rejoin yarn
and knit to end.

Complete to match first side,
reversing shapings.

LEFT FRONT:
Using 3.25mm needles cast on
41(41, 41, 45, 45, 49)sts.

Work in rib as given for back until left
front meas 6cm, dec(inc, inc, dec, inc,
dec) 1 st in centre of last row. 40[42, 42,
44, 46, 48]sts.

Change to 4mm needles, starting with
a K row work in st st until left front meas
23(26.5, 28, 30.5, 33.5, 34.5)cm, ending
with a WS row.

Shape armholes
Next Row: Cast off 3sts, knit to end.
37[39, 39, 41, 43, 45]sts.
Work 1 row.
Dec 1 st at armhole edge on next and 3
foll alt rows. 33[35, 35, 37, 39, 41]sts.

Cont straight until armhole meas 12cm,
ending with a RS row.

Shape neck
Next Row (WS): Cast off 8(8, 8, 8, 9, 9)sts,
purl to end. 25[27, 27, 29, 30, 32]sts.
Dec 1 st at neck edge on every row until
16(18, 18, 18, 18, 20)sts remain.
Cont straight until work matches length
of back, ending with a WS row.
Cast off.

RIGHT FRONT:
Work as given for left front reversing
all shapings.

SLEEVES:
Using 3.25mm needles cast on
37(37, 37, 37, 41, 41)sts.

Work in rib as given for back until sleeve
meas 6cm, dec 1 st in centre of last row,
ending with a WS row.
36[36, 36, 36, 40, 40]sts.

Change to 4mm needles, starting with a
K row work in st st, inc 1 st at each end
of next and every foll alt row to
44(44, 46, 46, 48, 48)sts then every foll
4th row to 74(74, 74, 78, 80, 80)sts.

Cont straight until work measures
27(28.5, 30, 31, 32, 34)cm, ending with a
WS row.

Shape sleeve top
Cast off 3sts at beg of next 2 rows.
68[68, 68, 72, 74, 74]sts.
Dec 1 st at each end of next and 3 foll alt
rows. 60[60, 60, 64, 66, 66]sts.
Work 1 row.
Cast off.

FINISHING:
Press as described on the
information page.
Join both shoulder seams.

Button band
With RS facing, using 3.25mm needles
beg at cast-off sts at neck edge pick up
and knit 80(88, 92, 100, 104, 104)sts
along left front edge.
Row 1: (WS) (P3, K1) to end.
Row 2: (P1, K3) to end.
Rep last 2 rows twice more.
Cast off in patt.

Button hole band
With RS facing, using 3.25mm needles
beg at lower edge pick up and knit
80(88, 92, 100, 104, 104)sts along right
front edge.

Row 1: (WS) (K1, P3) to end.
Row 2: (K3, P1) to end.
Row 3: * Patt 11(12, 13, 13, 15, 15)sts,
yrn, patt2tog, rep from * to last
2(4, 2, 4, 2, 2)sts, patt 2(4, 2, 4, 2, 2)sts .
Row 4: As row 2.
Row 5: As row 1.
Row 6: As row 2.
Cast off in patt.

Neck band:
With RS facing, using 3.25mm needles
starting at button hole band pick up 6sts
across button hole band, 15(15, 15, 16,
18, 18)sts up right side of front neck,
2sts down right side of back neck, knit
32(32, 32, 36, 40, 40)sts from back neck
holder, pick up and knit 2sts up left side
of back neck, 15(15, 15, 16, 18, 18)sts
down left side of front neck, and 6sts
across button band.
78[78, 78, 84, 92, 92]sts

Row 1: (WS) (P3, K1) to last
2(2, 2, 0, 0, 0)sts, P2(2, 2, 0, 0, 0) .
Row 2: K0(0, 0, 2, 2, 2)sts, (K3, P1)
to end.
Row 3: (P3, K1) to last 4sts, yrn,
patt2tog, patt to end.
Row 4: As row 2.
Row 5: As row 1.
Row 6: As row 2.
Cast off in patt.

Sew in sleeves.

Join side and sleeve seams.

Attach buttons.

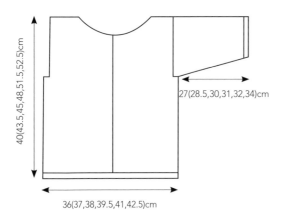

27(28.5,30,31,32,34)cm

40(43.5,45,48,51.5,52.5)cm

36(37,38,39.5,41,42.5)cm

Austin

v-neck sweater

SIZE: To fit age 4-5(5-6, 6-7, 7-8, 8-9, 9-10) years

YARN USAGE:
Rowan Summerlite DK shown in Linen 460 – 5(5, 5, 5, 6, 6) x 50g

NEEDLES:
3.25mm (US 3) and 4mm (US 6) needles

EXTRAS:
Stitch Holders

TENSION:
22sts and 30rows = 10cm
Measured over st st using 4mm needles

BACK:
Using 3.25mm needles, cast on 81(85, 85, 89, 93, 97)sts.

Row 1: (RS) P1, (K3, P1) to end.
Row 2: (K1, P3) to last st, K1.
These 2 rows form rib.

Rep last 2 rows until back meas 6cm, dec 1 st in centre of last row, ending with a WS row. 80[84, 84, 88, 92, 96]sts.

Change to 4mm needles, starting with a K row work in st st until back meas 23(26.5,28, 30.5, 33.5, 34.5)cm, ending with a WS row.

Shape armholes
Cast off 3sts at beg of next 2 rows. 74[78, 78, 82, 86, 90]sts.

Dec 1 st at each end of next and 3 foll alt rows. 66[70, 70, 74, 78, 82]sts. **

Cont straight until armhole meas 17(17, 17, 17.5, 18, 18)cm, ending with a WS row.

Shape back neck
Next Row: K17(19, 19, 19, 19, 21) turn,
leaving rem sts on a stitch holder.
Work each side of neck separately.
Dec 1 st at neck edge on next row.
16[18, 18, 18, 18, 20]sts.
Cast off.

With RS facing, slip centre 32(32, 32, 36,
40, 40)sts onto a stitch holder, rejoin yarn
and knit to end.

Complete to match first side,
reversing shapings.

FRONT:
Work as given for back to **.
Cont straight until armhole meas 7cm,
ending with a WS row.

Divide for neck
Next Row: K33(35, 35, 37, 39, 41) turn,
leaving rem sts on a stitch holder.

Work each side of neck separately.

Dec 1 st at neck edge on next 11(11, 11,
13, 15, 15) rows then on every foll alt row
until 16(18, 18, 18, 18, 20)sts remain.

Cont straight until work matches length
of back, ending with a WS row.

Cast off.

With RS facing, rejoin yarn to rem sts and
knit to end.

Complete to match first side.

SLEEVES:
Using 3.25mm needles cast on
37(37, 37, 37, 41, 41)sts.
Work in rib as given for back until sleeve
meas 6cm, dec 1 st in centre of last row,
ending with a WS row.
36[36, 36, 36, 40, 40]sts.

Change to 4mm needles, starting with a
K row work in st st, inc 1 st at each end
of next and every foll alt row to 44(44,
46, 46, 48, 48)sts, then every foll 4th row
to 74(74, 74, 78, 80, 80)sts.

Cont straight until work measures
27(28.5, 30, 31, 32, 34)cm, ending with a
WS row.

Shape sleeve top
Cast off 3sts at beg of next 2 rows.
68[68, 68, 72, 74, 74]sts.
Dec 1 st at each end of next and 3 foll alt
rows. 60[60, 60,64, 66, 66]sts.
Work 1 row.
Cast off.

FINISHING:
Press as described on the
information page.
Join right shoulder seam.

Neckband
With RS facing, using 3.25mm needles,
pick up 32(32, 32, 34, 34, 34)sts down
left front neck, 32(32, 32, 34, 34, 34)sts
up right front neck, 2sts from right back
neck, knit 32(32, 32, 36, 40, 40)sts from
back neck holder and 2sts up left back
neck. 100[100, 100, 108, 112, 112]sts.

Row 1: (WS) (P3, K1) 15(15, 15, 18, 19, 19)times, P12, (K1, P3) to end.
Row 2: (K3, P1) 7 times, K4, (K2tog) twice, K4, (P1, K3) to end.
Row 3: (P3, K1) 15(15, 15, 18, 19, 19) times, P3, (P2tog) twice, P3, (K1, P3) to end.
Row 4: (K3, P1) 7 times, K2, (K2tog) twice, K2, (P1, K3) to end.
Row 5: (P3, K1) 15(15, 15, 18, 19, 19) times, P1, (P2tog) twice, P1, (K1, P3) to end.
Row 6: (K3, P1) 7 times, (K2tog) twice, (P1, K3) to end.
Cast off in patt.

Join left shoulder and neckband seams.

Sew in sleeves.

Join side and sleeve seams.

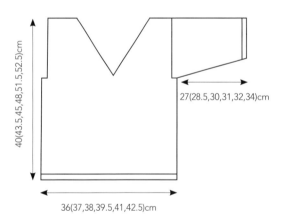

40(43.5,45,48,51.5,52.5)cm

27(28.5,30,31,32,34)cm

36(37,38,39.5,41,42.5)cm

HeNRY

cable sweater

SIZE: To fit age 4-5(5-6, 6-7, 7-8, 8-9, 9-10) years

YARN USAGE:
Rowan Summerlite 4ply
shown in Still Grey 422
4(5, 5, 5, 6, 6) x 50g

NEEDLES:
3mm (US 2) and 3.25mm (US 3) needles

EXTRAS:
Cable needle
Stitch holder

TENSION:
32sts and 36rows = 10cm
Measured over cable pattern using
3.25mm needles

SPECIAL ABBREVIATIONS
C6B: Slip 3sts onto cable needle and
hold at back of work, K3, then K3 from
cable needle.

BACK:
Using 3mm needles cast on 111(115, 117, 119, 125, 129)sts.
Row 1: (RS) (K1, P1) to last st, K1.
Row 2: (P1, K1) to last st, P1.
These 2 rows form rib.
Row 8: Rib to end, inc 7sts evenly across the row. 118[122, 124, 126, 132, 136]sts.

Change to 3.25mm needles.

4-5 years only
Row 1: K2, P2, K6, P2, * K3, P2, K6, P2, rep from * to last 2sts, K2.
Row 2: P2, * K2, P6, K2, P3, rep from * to last 12sts, K2, P6, K2, P2.
Row 3: K2, P2, C6B, P2, * K3, P2, C6B, P2, rep from * to last 2sts, K2.
Row 4: As row 2.
Row 5: As row 1.
Row 6: As row 2.
Rows 1 to 6 form patt.

5-6 years only
Row 1: P1, * K3, P2, K6, P2, rep from * to last 4sts, K3, P1.
Row 2: K1, P3, * K2, P6, K2, P3 rep from * to last st, K1.
Row 3: P1, * K3, P2, C6B, P2, rep from * to last 4sts, K3, P1.
Row 4: As row 2.
Row 5: As row 1.
Row 6: As row 2.
Rows 1 to 6 form patt.

6-7 years only
Row 1: P2, * K3, P2, K6, P2, rep from * to last 5sts, K3, P2.
Row 2: K2, P3, * K2, P6, K2, P3, rep from * to last 2sts, K2.
Row 3: P2, * K3, P2, C6B, P2, rep from * to last 5sts, K3, P2.
Row 4: As row 2.
Row 5: As row 1.
Row 6: As row 2.
Rows 1 to 6 form patt.

7-8 years only
Row 1: K1, P2, * K3, P2, K6, P2, rep from * to last 6sts, K3, P2, K1.
Row 2: P1, K2, P3, * K2, P6, K2, P3, rep from * to last 3sts, K2, P1.
Row 3: K1, P2, * K3, P2, C6B, P2, rep from * to last 6sts, K3, P2, K1.
Row 4: As row 2.
Row 5: As row 1.
Row 6: As row 2.
Rows 1 to 6 form patt.

8-9 years only
Row 1: K4, P2, * K3, P2, K6, P2, rep from * to last 9sts, K3, P2, K4.
Row 2: P4, K2, P3 * K2, P6, K2, P3, rep from * to last 6sts, K2, P4.
Row 3: K4, P2, * K3, P2, C6B, P2, rep from * to last 9sts, K3, P2, K4.
Row 4: As row 2.
Row 5: As row 1.
Row 6: As row 2.
Rows 1 to 6 form patt.

9-10 years only
Row 1: K6, P2, * K3, P2, K6, P2, rep from * to last 11sts, K3, P2, K6.
Row 2: P6, K2, P3, * K2, P6, K2, P3, rep from * to last 8sts, K2, P6.
Row 3: K6, P2, * K3, P2, C6B, P2, rep from * to last 11sts, K3, P2, K6.
Row 4: As row 2.
Row 5: As row 1.
Row 6: As row 2.
Rows 1 to 6 form patt.

For all sizes
Cont in patt until back meas 23(26.5, 28, 30.5, 33.5, 34.5)cm, ending with a WS row.

Shape armholes
Keeping patt correct cast off 3sts at beg of next 2 rows.
112[116, 118, 120, 126, 130]sts.
Dec 1 st at each end of next and 4 foll rows. 102[106, 108, 110, 116, 120]sts.
Dec 1 st at each end of next and 2 foll alt rows. 96[100, 102, 104, 110, 114]sts. **

Cont straight until armhole meas 17(17, 17, 17.5, 18, 18)cm, ending with a WS row.

Shape back neck
Next row: Patt 26(28, 28, 29, 31, 32) turn, leaving rem sts on a stitch holder. Work each side of neck separately. Dec 1 st at neck edge on next row. 25[27, 27, 28, 30, 31]sts.
Cast off.

With RS facing, slip centre 44(44, 46, 46, 48, 50)sts onto a stitch holder, rejoin yarn and patt to end.

Complete to match first side, reversing shapings.

FRONT:
Work as given for back to **.
Cont straight until armhole meas 12cm, ending with a WS row.

Shape neck
Next row: Patt 38(39, 40, 40, 43, 44) turn, leaving rem sts on a stitch holder. Work each side of neck separately.
Next row: Cast off 2sts, patt to end. 36[37, 38, 38, 41, 42]sts.
Dec 1 st at neck edge on next 9 rows. 27[28, 29, 29, 32, 33]sts.
Dec 1 st at neck edge on every foll alt row until 25(27, 27, 28, 30, 31)sts remain.
Cont straight until work matches length of back, ending with a WS row.
Cast off.

With RS facing, slip centre 20(22, 22, 24, 24, 26)sts onto a stitch holder, rejoin yarn and patt to end. Complete to match first side, reversing shapings.

SLEEVES:
Using 3mm needles, cast on 53sts.
Work 7 rows in rib as given for Back.
Row 8: Rib to end, inc 6sts evenly across row. [59sts].

Change to 3.25mm needles, work in patt as folls:

Cont in patt inc 1 st at each end of next and every alt row to 77sts and every foll 4th row to 107 (107, 107, 111, 115, 115) sts, taking increased sts into patt.

Row 1: (RS) P2, * K3, P2, K6, P2 rep from * to last 5sts, K3, P2.
Row 2: K2, P3, *K2, P6, K2, P3 rep from* to last 2sts, K2.
Row 3: P2, * K3, P2, C6B, P2, rep from * to last 5sts, K3, P2.
Row 4: As row 2.
Row 5: As row 1.
Row 6: As row 2.
Rows 1 to 6 form patt.

Cont straight until sleeve meas 27(28.5, 30, 31, 32, 34)cm, ending with a WS row.

Shape sleeve top
Keeping patt correct cast off 3sts at beg of next 2 rows. 101[101, 101, 105, 109, 109]sts.
Dec 1 st at each end of next and 4 foll rows. 91[91, 91, 95, 99, 99]sts.
Dec 1 st at each end of 2nd and 2 foll alt rows. 85[85, 85, 89, 93, 93]sts.
Work 1 row.
Cast off.

FINISHING:

Press as described on the information page.
Join right shoulder seam.

Neckband

With RS facing, using 3mm needles pick up and knit 16sts down left side of front neck, knit 20(22, 22, 24, 24, 26)sts across front neck holder, pick up and knit 17sts up right side of front neck, pick up 2sts down right side of back neck, knit 44(44, 46, 46, 48, 50)sts across back neck holder, and pick up and knit 2sts up left side of back neck.
101[103, 105, 107, 109, 113]sts.

Row 1: (WS) P1, (K1, P1) to end.
Row 2: K1, (P1, K1) to end.
Rep last 2 rows once more.
Cast off.

Join left shoulder and neck band seams.

Sew in sleeves.

Join side and sleeve seams.

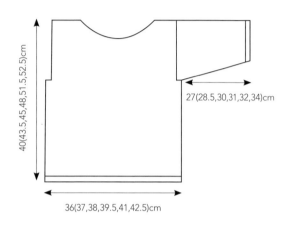

40(43.5,45,48,51.5,52.5)cm

27(28.5,30,31,32,34)cm

36(37,38,39.5,41,42.5)cm

POPPY

cable cardigan

SIZE: To fit age 4-5(5-6, 6-7, 7-8, 8-9, 9-10) years

YARN USAGE:
Rowan Summerlite 4ply
shown in Pinched Pink 426
4(4, 5, 5, 5, 6) x 50g

NEEDLES:
3mm (US 2) and 3.25mm (US 3) needles

EXTRAS:
Cable needle
Stitch Holder
5(5, 5, 6, 6, 6) x Buttons

TENSION:
32sts and 36rows = 10 rows
Measured over pattern using
3.25mm needles

SPECIAL ABBREVIATIONS
C6B - Slip 3sts onto cable needle and hold at back of work, K3, then K3 from cable needle.

BACK:
Using 3mm needles cast on 111(115, 117, 119, 125, 129)sts.
Row 1: (RS) (K1, P1) to last st, K1.
Row 2: (P1, K1) to last st, P1.
These 2 rows form rib.
Work 5 rows in rib.
Row 8: Rib to end, inc 7sts evenly across the row. 118[122, 124, 126, 132, 136]sts.

Change to 3.25mm needles.

4-5 years only
Row 1: K2, P2, K6, P2, * K3, P2, K6, P2 rep from * to last 2sts, K2.
Row 2: P2, * K2, P6, K2, P3 rep from * to last 12sts, K2, P6, K2, P2.
Row 3: K2, P2, C6B, P2, * K3, P2, C6B, P2 rep from * to last 2sts, K2.
Row 4: As row 2.
Row 5: As row 1.
Row 6: As row 2.
Rows 1 to 6 form patt.

5-6 years only
Row 1: P1 * K3, P2, K6, P2, rep from * to last 4sts, K3, P1.
Row 2: K1, P3, * K2, P6, K2, P3 rep from * to last st, K1.
Row 3: P1 * K3, P2, C6B, P2, rep from * to last 4sts, K3, P1.
Row 4: As row 2.
Row 5: As row 1.
Row 6: As row 2.
Rows 1 to 6 form patt.

6-7 years only
Row 1: P2, * K3, P2, K6, P2, rep from * to last 5sts, K3, P2.
Row 2: K2, P3, * K2, P6, K2, P3, rep from * to last 2sts, K2.
Row 3: P2, * K3, P2, C6B, P2, rep from * to last 5sts, K3, P2.
Row 4: As row 2.
Row 5: As row 1.
Row 6: As row 2.
Rows 1 to 6 form patt.

7-8 years only
Row 1: K1, P2, * K3, P2, K6, P2, rep from * to last 6sts, K3, P2, K1.
Row 2: P1, K2, P3, * K2, P6, K2, P3, rep from * to last 3sts, K2, P1.
Row 3: K1, P2, * K3, P2, C6B, P2, rep from * to last 6sts, K3, P2, K1.
Row 4: As row 2.
Row 5: As row 1.
Row 6: As row 2.
Rows 1 to 6 form patt.

8-9 years only
Row 1: K4, P2, * K3, P2, K6, P2, rep from * to last 9sts, K3, P2, K4.
Row 2: P4, K2, P3 * K2, P6, K2, P3, rep from * to last 6sts, K2, P4.
Row 3: K4, P2, * K3, P2, C6B, P2, rep from * to last 9sts, K3, P2, K4.
Row 4: As row 2.
Row 5: As row 1.
Row 6: As row 2.
Rows 1 to 6 form patt.

9-10 years only
Row 1: K6, P2, * K3, P2, K6, P2, rep from * to last 11sts, K3, P2, K6.
Row 2: P6, K2, P3, *K2, P6, K2, P3, rep from * to last 8sts, K2, P6.
Row 3: K6, P2, * K3, P2, C6B, P2, rep from * to last 11sts, K3, P2, K6.
Row 4: As row 2.
Row 5: As row 1.
Row 6: As row 2.
Rows 1 to 6 form patt.

For all sizes
Cont in patt until back meas 23(26.5, 28, 30.5, 33.5, 34.5)cm, ending with a WS row.

Shape armholes
Keeping patt correct cast off 3sts at beg of next 2 rows.
112[116, 118, 120, 126, 130]sts.
Dec 1 st at each end of next and 4 foll rows. 102[106, 108, 110, 116, 120]sts.
Dec 1 st at each end of 2nd and 2 foll alt rows. 96[100, 102, 104, 110, 114]sts.

Cont straight until armhole meas 17(17, 17, 17.5, 18, 18)cm, ending with a WS row.

Shape back neck
Next row: Patt 26(28, 28, 29, 31, 32) turn, leaving rem sts on a stitch holder.
Work each side of neck separately.
Dec 1 st at neck edge on next row.
25[27, 27, 28, 30, 31]sts.
Cast off.

With RS facing, slip centre 44(44, 46, 46, 48, 50)sts onto a stitch holder, rejoin yarn and patt to end.
Complete to match first side, reversing shapings.

LEFT FRONT:
Using 3mm needles cast on 56(58, 58, 60, 62, 64)sts.
Row 1: (RS) * K1, P1, rep from * to end.
This row forms rib.
Work 6 rows in rib.
Row 8: Rib to end, inc 3(3, 4, 3, 4, 4) sts evenly across row.
59[61, 62, 63, 66, 68]sts.

Change to 3.25mm needles.

4-5 years only
Row 1: K2, P2, K6, P2, * K3, P2, K6, P2, rep from * to last 8 sts, K3, P2, K3.
Row 2: P3, K2, P3, * K2, P6, K2, P3, rep from * to last 12sts, K2, P6, K2, P2.
Row 3: K2, P2, C6B, P2, * K3, P2, C6B, P2, rep from * to last 8 sts, K3, P2, K3.
Row 4: As row 2.
Row 5: As row 1.
Row 6: As row 2.
Rows 1 to 6 form patt.

5-6 years only
Row 1: P1,* K3, P2, K6, P2, rep from * to last 8 sts, K3, P2, K3.
Row 2: P3, K2, P3, * K2, P6, K2, P3, rep from * to last st, K1.
Row 3: P1,* K3, P2, C6B, P2, rep from * to last 8 sts, K3, P2, K3.

Row 4: As row 2.
Row 5: As row 1.
Row 6: As row 2.
Rows 1 to 6 form patt.

6-7 years only
Row 1: P2, * K3, P2, K6, P2, rep from * to last 8 sts, K3, P2, K3.
Row 2: P3, K2, P3 * K2, P6, K2, P3, rep from * to last 2sts, K2.
Row 3: P2, * K3, P2, C6B, P2, rep from * to last 8 sts, K3, P2, K3.
Row 4: As row 2.
Row 5: As row 1.
Row 6: As row 2.
Rows 1 to 6 form patt.

7-8 years only
Row 1: K1, P2, * K3, P2, K6, P2, rep from * to last 8 sts, K3, P2, K3.
Row 2: P3, K2, P3, * K2, P6, K2, P3, rep from * to last 3sts, K2, P1.
Row 3: K1, P2, * K3, P2, C6B, P2, rep from * to last 8 sts, K3, P2, K3.
Row 4: As row 2.
Row 5: As row 1.
Row 6: As row 2.
Rows 1 to 6 form patt.

8-9 years only
Row 1: K4, P2, * K3, P2, K6, P2, rep from * to last 8 sts, K3, P2, K3.
Row 2: P3, K2, P3, * K2, P6, K2, P3, rep from * to last 6sts, K2, P4.
Row 3: K4, P2, * K3, P2, C6B, P2, rep from * to last 8 sts, K3, P2, K3.
Row 4: As row 2.
Row 5: As row 1.
Row 6: As row 2.
Rows 1 to 6 form patt.

9-10 years only
Row 1: K6, P2, * K3, P2, K6, P2, rep from * to last 8 sts, K3, P2, K3.
Row 2: P3, K2, P3, *K2, P6, K2, P3, rep from * to last 8sts, K2, P6.
Row 3: K6, P2, * K3, P2, C6B, P2, rep from * to last 8 sts, K3, P2, K3.
Row 4: As row 2.
Row 5: As row 1.

Row 6: As row 2.
Rows 1 to 6 form patt.

For all sizes
Cont in patt until left front meas 23(26.5, 28, 30.5, 33.5, 34.5)cm, ending with a WS row.

Shape armhole
Keeping patt correct cast off 3sts at beg of next row, 56[58, 59, 60, 63, 65]sts.
Work 1 row.
Dec 1 st at armhole edge on next and 4 foll rows. 51[53, 54, 55, 58, 60]sts.
Dec 1 st at armhole edge on 2nd and 2 foll alt row. 48[50, 51, 52, 55, 57]sts.
Cont straight until armhole meas 12cm, ending with a RS row.

Shape neck
Next Row: Cast off 10sts, patt to end.
38[40, 41, 42, 45, 47]sts.
Dec 1 st at neck edge on every row until 25(27, 27, 28, 30, 31)sts remain.
Cont straight until work matches same length as back, ending with a WS row.
Cast off.

RIGHT FRONT:
Using 3mm needles cast on 56(58, 58, 60, 62, 64)sts.
Row 1: (RS) * P1, K1, rep from * to end.
This row forms rib.
Work 6 rows in rib.
Row 8: Rib to end, inc 3(3, 4, 3, 4, 4) sts evenly across row.
59[61, 62, 63, 66, 68]sts.

Change to 3.25mm needles.

4-5 years only
Row 1: K3, P2, * K3, P2, K6, P2, rep from * to last 2sts, K2.
Row 2: P2, *K2, P6, K2, P3, rep from * to last 5sts, K2, P3.
Row 3: K3, P2,* K3, P2, C6B, P2 rep from * to last 2sts, K2.
Row 4: As row 2.
Row 5: As row 1.
Row 6: As row 2.
Rows 1 to 6 form patt.

5-6 years only
Row 1: K3, P2, * K3, P2, K6, P2, rep from * to last 4sts, K3, P1.
Row 2: K1, P3, * K2, P6, K2, P3, rep from * to last 5sts, K2, P3.
Row 3: K3, P2 * K3, P2, C6B, P2, rep from * to last 4sts, K3, P1.
Row 4: As row 2.
Row 5: As row 1.
Row 6: As row 2.
Rows 1 to 6 form patt.

6-7 years only
Row 1: K3, P2, * K3, P2, K6, P2, rep from * to last 5sts, K3, P2.
Row 2: K2, P3, * K2, P6, K2, P3, rep from * to last 5sts, K2, P3.
Row 3: K3, P2, * K3, P2, C6B, P2, rep from * to last 5sts, K3, P2.
Row 4: As row 2.
Row 5: As row 1.
Row 6: As row 2.
Rows 1 to 6 form patt.

7-8 years only
Row 1: K3, P2, * K3, P2, K6, P2, rep from * to last 6sts, K3, P2, K1.
Row 2: P1, K2, P3, * K2, P6, K2, P3, rep from * to last 5sts, K2, P3.
Row 3: K3, P2, * K3, P2, C6B, P2, rep from * to last 6sts, K3, P2, K1.
Row 4: As row 2.
Row 5: As row 1.
Row 6: As row 2.
Rows 1 to 6 form patt.

8-9 years only
Row 1: K3, P2, * K3, P2, K6, P2, rep from * to last 9sts, K3, P2, K4.
Row 2: P4, K2, P3, * K2, P6, K2, P3, rep from * to last 5sts, K2, P3.
Row 3: K3, P2, * K3, P2, C6B, P2, rep from * to last 9sts, K3, P2, K4.
Row 4: As row 2.
Row 5: As row 1.
Row 6: As row 2.
Rows 1 to 6 form patt.

9-10 years only
Row 1: K3, P2, * K3, P2, K6, P2, rep from * to last 11sts, K3, P2, K6.
Row 2: P6, K2, P3, * K2, P6, K2, P3, rep from * to last 5sts, K2, P3.
Row 3: K3, P2,* K3, P2, C6B, P2, rep from * to last 11sts, K3, P2, K6.
Row 4: As row 2.
Row 5: As row 1.
Row 6: As row 2.
Rows 1 to 6 form patt.

For all sizes
Cont in patt until right front meas 23(26.5, 28, 30.5, 33.5, 34.5)cm, ending with a RS row.

Shape armhole
Keeping patt correct cast off 3sts at beg of next row. 56[58, 59, 60, 63, 65]sts.
Dec 1 st at armhole edge on next and 4 foll rows. 51[53, 54, 55, 58, 60]sts.
Dec 1 st at armhole edge on 2nd and 2 foll alt row. 48[50, 51, 52, 55, 57]sts.

Cont in patt until armhole meas 12cm, ending with a WS row.

Shape neck
Next Row: Cast off 10sts, patt to end. 38[40, 41, 42, 45, 47]sts.
Work 1 row.
Dec 1 st at neck edge on every row until 25(27, 27, 28, 30, 31)sts remain.
Cont in patt until work matches same length as back, ending with a RS row.
Cast off.

SLEEVES:
Using 3mm needles cast on 53sts.
Work 7 rows in rib as given for Back.
Row 8: Rib to end, inc 6sts evenly across row. [59sts].

Change to 3.25mm needles.

Cont in patt inc 1 st at each end of next and every alt row to 77sts and every foll 4th row to 107 (107, 107, 111, 115, 115) sts, taking increased sts into patt.

Row 1: (RS) P2, * K3, P2, K6, P2, rep from * to last 5sts, K3, P2.
Row 2: K2, P3, * K2, P6, K2, P3, rep from * to last 2sts, K2.
Row 3: P2, * K3, P2, C6B, P2, rep from * to last 5sts, K3, P2.
Row 4: As row 2.
Row 5: As row 1.
Row 6: As row 2.
Rows 1 to 6 form patt.

Cont in patt until sleeve meas 27(28.5, 30, 31, 32, 34)cm, ending with a WS row.

Shape sleeve top
Keeping patt correct cast off 3sts at beg of next 2 rows.
101[101, 101, 105, 109, 109]sts.
Dec 1 st at each end of next and 4 foll rows. 91[91, 91, 95, 99, 99]sts.
Dec 1 st at each end of 2nd and 2 foll alt rows. 85[85, 85, 89, 93, 93]sts.
Work 1 row.
Cast off.

FINISHING:
Press as described on the information page.
Join both shoulder seams.

Button hole band:
With RS facing, using 3mm needles beg at lower edge pick up and knit 104(114, 114, 124, 136, 142)sts along right front edge.
Row 1: (WS) (K1, P1) to end.
Row 2: (K1, P1) to end.
Row 3: *Patt 18(20, 20, 22, 20, 21)sts, yrn, patt 2 tog, rep from * 4(4, 4, 5, 5, 5) times more, patt to end.
Row 4: P1, K1 to end.
Rep last row 2 times more.
Cast off in rib.

Button band
With RS facing, using 3mm needles beg at cast-off sts at neck edge pick up and knit 104(114, 114, 124, 136, 142)sts along left front edge.

Row 1: (WS) (P1, K1) to end.
Rep last row 5 times more.
Cast off in rib.

Neck band
With RS facing, using 3mm needles
starting at button hole band pick up and
knit 6sts across button hole band, 23sts
up right side of front neck, 2sts down
right side of back neck, knit 44(44, 46,
46, 48, 50)sts across back neck holder,
pick up and knit 2sts up left side of back
neck, 24sts down left side of front neck,
and 6sts across button band.
107[107, 109, 109, 111, 113]sts.

Row 1: (WS) P1, (K1, P1) to end.
Row 2: K1, P1, K1, yrn, patt 2 tog,
(P1, K1) to end.
Row 3: P1, (K1, P1) to end.
Row 4: K1, (P1, K1) to end.
Rep last 2 rows once more.
Cast off in rib.

Sew in sleeves.

Join side and sleeve seams.

Attach buttons.

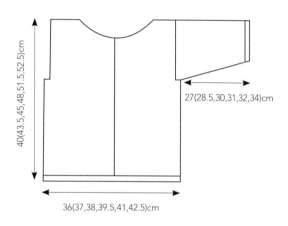

40(43.5,45,48,51.5,52.5)cm

27(28.5,30,31,32,34)cm

36(37,38,39.5,41,42.5)cm

edWARd

cable tank top

SIZE: To fit age 4-5(5-6, 6-7, 7-8, 8-9, 9-10) years

YARN USAGE:
Rowan Summerlite 4ply
shown in Duck Egg 419
3(3, 3, 4, 4, 4) x 50g

NEEDLES:
3mm (US 2) and 3.25mm (US 3) needles

EXTRAS:
Cable needle
Stitch Holder

TENSION:
32sts and 36rows = 10cm
Measured over pattern using
3.25mm needles

SPECIAL ABBREVIATIONS
C6B - Slip 3sts onto cable needle and
hold at back of work, K3, then K3 from
cable needle.

BACK:
Using 3mm needles cast on 111(115, 117, 119, 125, 129)sts.
Row 1: (RS) (K1, P1) to last st, K1.
Row 2: (P1, K1) to last st, P1.
These 2 rows form rib.
Work 5 rows in rib.
Row 8: Rib to end, inc 7sts evenly across the row. 118[122, 124, 126, 132, 136]sts.

Change to 3.25mm needles, work in patt as folls:

4-5 years only
Row 1: K2, P2, K6, P2, * K3, P2, K6, P2 rep from * to last 2sts, K2.
Row 2: P2, * K2, P6, K2, P3 rep from * to last 12sts, K2, P6, K2, P2.
Row 3: K2, P2, C6B, P2, * K3, P2, C6B, P2 rep from * to last 2sts, K2.
Row 4: As row 2.
Row 5: As row 1.

Row 6: As row 2.
Rows 1 to 6 form patt.

5-6 years only
Row 1: P1 * K3, P2, K6, P2, rep from * to last 4sts, K3, P1.
Row 2: K1, P3, * K2, P6, K2, P3 rep from * to last st, K1.
Row 3: P1 * K3, P2, C6B, P2, rep from * to last 4sts, K3, P1.
Row 4: As row 2.
Row 5: As row 1.
Row 6: As row 2.
Rows 1 to 6 form patt.

6-7 years only
Row 1: P2, * K3, P2, K6, P2, rep from * to last 5sts, K3, P2.
Row 2: K2, P3, * K2, P6, K2, P3, rep from * to last 2sts, K2.
Row 3: P2, * K3, P2, C6B, P2, rep from * to last 5sts, K3, P2.
Row 4: As row 2.
Row 5: As row 1.
Row 6: As row 2.
Rows 1 to 6 form patt.

7-8 years only
Row 1: K1, P2, * K3, P2, K6, P2, rep from * to last 6sts, K3, P2, K1.
Row 2: P1, K2, P3, *K2, P6, K2, P3, rep from * to last 3sts, K2, P1.
Row 3: K1, P2, * K3, P2, C6B, P2, rep from * to last 6sts, K3, P2, K1.
Row 4: As row 2.
Row 5: As row 1.
Row 6: As row 2.
Rows 1 to 6 form patt.

8-9 years only
Row 1: K4, P2, * K3, P2, K6, P2, rep from * to last 9sts, K3, P2, K4.
Row 2: P4, K2, P3 * K2, P6, K2, P3, rep from * to last 6sts, K2, P4.
Row 3: K4, P2, * K3, P2, C6B, P2, rep from * to last 9sts, K3, P2, K4.
Row 4: As row 2.
Row 5: As row 1.
Row 6: As row 2.
Rows 1 to 6 form patt.

9-10 years only
Row 1: K6, P2, * K3, P2, K6, P2, rep from * to last 11sts, K3, P2, K6.
Row 2: P6, K2, P3, * K2, P6, K2, P3, rep from * to last 8sts, K2, P6.
Row 3: K6, P2, * K3, P2, C6B, P2, rep from * to last 11sts, K3, P2, K6.
Row 4: As row 2.
Row 5: As row 1.
Row 6: As row 2.
Rows 1 to 6 form patt.

For all sizes
Cont in patt until back meas 23(26.5, 28, 30.5, 33.5, 34.5)cm, ending with a WS row.

Shape armholes
Keeping patt correct cast off 3sts at beg of next 2 rows. 112[116, 118, 120, 126, 130]sts.
Dec 1 st at each end of next and 4 foll rows. 102[106, 108, 110, 116, 120]sts.
Dec 1 st at each end of 2nd and 2 foll alt rows. 96[100, 102, 104, 110, 114]sts. **

Cont straight until armhole meas 17(17, 17, 17.5, 18, 18)cm, ending with a WS row.

Shape back neck
Next row: Patt 26(28, 28, 29, 31, 32) turn, leaving rem sts on a stitch holder. Work each side of neck separately.
Dec 1 st at neck edge on next row. 25[27, 27, 28, 30, 31]sts.
Cast off.

With RS facing, slip centre 44(44, 46, 46, 48, 50)sts onto a stitch holder, rejoin yarn and patt to end.

Complete to match first side, reversing shapings.

FRONT:
Work as given for back to **.
Cont straight until armhole meas 7cm, ending with a WS row.

Divide for neck
Next Row: Patt 48(50, 51, 52, 55, 57) turn, leaving rem sts on a stitch holder. Work each side of neck separately.
Next row: Cast off 2sts, patt to end. 46[48, 49, 50, 53, 55]sts.
Dec 1 st at neck edge on next 10 rows. 36[38, 39, 40, 43, 45]sts.
Dec 1 st at neck edge on next and every foll alt row until 25(27, 27, 28, 30, 31)sts remain.
Cont straight until work matches length of back, ending with a WS row.
Cast off.

With RS facing, rejoin yarn to rem sts and patt to end.

Complete to match first side, reversing shapings.
Cast off.

FINISHING:
Press as described on the information page.
Join right shoulder seam.

Neck band:
With RS facing, using 3mm needles pick up and knit 34sts down left side of front neck, 34sts up right side of front neck, 2sts down right side of back neck, knit 44[44, 46, 46, 48, 50]sts from back neck holder, and pick up and knit 2sts up left side of back neck. 116[116, 118, 118, 120, 122]sts.

Row 1: (WS) (P1, K1) 39(39, 40, 40, 41, 42) times, P8, (K1, P1) to end.
Row 2: (K1, P1) 15 times, K2, (K2tog) twice, K2, (P1, K1) to end.
Row 3: (P1, K1) 39(39, 40, 40, 41, 42) times, P6, (K1, P1) to end.
Row 4: (K1, P1) 15 times, K1, (K2tog) twice, K1, (P1, K1) to end.
Row 5: (P1, K1) 39(39, 40, 40, 41, 42) times, P4, (K1, P1) to end.
Row 6: (K1, P1) 15 times, (K2tog) twice, (P1, K1) to end.
Cast off in patt.

Join left shoulder and neck band seams.

Armbands (Both alike):
With RS facing, using 3mm needles pick up and knit 65[65, 69, 69, 73, 73]sts evenly all round armhole edge.
Beg with 2nd row of rib as given for Back work 4 rows. Cast off.

Join side and armband seams.

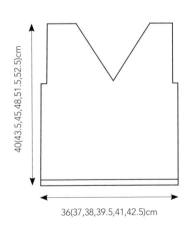

40(43.5,45,48,51.5,52.5)cm

36(37,38,39.5,41,42.5)cm

ALice

striped sweater

SIZE: To fit age 4-5(5-6, 6-7, 7-8, 8-9, 9-10) years

YARN USAGE:
Rowan Cotton Glace
A – shown in Bleached 726
4(4, 5, 5, 5, 6) x 50g

B – shown in Nightshade 746
2(2, 2, 2, 3, 3) x 50g

NEEDLES:
3mm (US 2) and 3.25mm (US 3) needles

EXTRAS:
Stitch Holders

TENSION:
23sts and 32rows = 10cms
measured over st st using
3.25mm needles

MOSS STITCH PATTERN:
Row 1: (K1, P1) to end.
Row 2: (P1, K1) to end.
Rep these 2 rows.

BACK:
Using 3mm needles and Yarn A, cast on
84(86, 88, 90, 94, 98)sts.
Work 8 rows in moss st patt, ending with
a WS row.

STRIPE PATTERN
Rows 1 & 2: A
Rows 3 & 4: B
Rows 5 – 8: A
Rows 9 & 10: B

Change to 3.25mm needles, starting
with a K row and keeping stripe pattern
correct work 10 rows in st st, repeating
rows 5 to 10 throughout cont in st st

until back meas 23(26.5, 28, 30.5, 33.5, 34.5)cm, ending with a WS row.

Shape Armholes
Cast off 3sts at beg of next 2 rows.
78[80, 82, 84, 88, 92]sts.
Dec 1 st at each end of next and 4 foll alt rows. 68[70, 72, 74, 78, 82]sts.

Cont straight until armhole meas approx 8 cm, ending with row 10 of stripe sequence.**

Break off yarn B and cont in yarn A only until armhole meas 17(17, 17, 17.5, 18, 18)cm, ending with a WS row.

Shape back neck
Next Row: K18(18, 19, 20, 18, 20) turn, leaving rem sts on a stitch holder.
Work each side of neck separately.
Dec 1 st at neck edge on next row.
17[17, 18, 19, 17, 19]sts.
Cast off.

With RS facing, slip centre 32(34, 34, 34, 42, 42)sts onto a stitch holder, rejoin yarn A and knit to end.
Complete to match first side, reversing shapings.

FRONT:
Work as given for back to **.
Break off yarn B and cont in yarn A only until armhole meas 12cm, ending with a WS row.

Shape neck
Next Row: K26(26, 27, 28, 26, 28) turn, leaving rem sts on a stitch holder.

Work each side of neck separately.

Next row: Cast off 2sts, purl to end.
24[24, 25, 26, 24, 26]sts.
Dec 1 st at neck edge on next 7 rows.
17[17, 18, 19, 17, 19]sts.

Cont straight until work matches length of back, ending with a WS row.

Cast off.

With RS facing, slip centre 16(18, 18, 18, 26, 26)sts onto a stitch holder, rejoin yarn A and knit to end.

Complete to match first side, reversing shapings.

SLEEVES:
Using 3mm needles and Yarn A, cast on 38(38, 38, 40, 40, 42)sts.
Work 8 rows in moss st patt as given for back.

Change to 3.25mm needles, starting with a K row and keeping stripe sequence correct work 10 rows in st st **AT THE SAME TIME** inc 1 st at each end of next and 2 foll 4th rows.
44[44, 44, 46, 46, 48]sts.

Cont in st st repeating rows 5 – 10 throughout **AT THE SAME TIME** inc 1 st at each end of 3rd and every foll 4th row until 74(78, 78, 80, 82, 82)sts.

Cont straight until sleeve meas approx
27(28.5, 30, 31, 32, 34)cm, ending with
row 10 of stripe sequence.
Break off yarn B and cont in yarn A only.

Shape sleeve top
Cast off 3sts at beg of next 2 rows.
72[72, 72, 74, 76, 76]sts.
Dec 1 st at each end of next and 4 foll
alt rows. 62[62, 62, 64, 66, 66]sts.
Work 1 row.
Cast off.

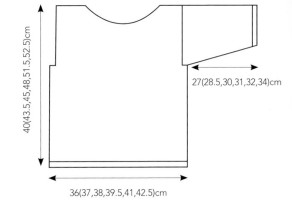

40(43.5,45,48,51.5,52.5)cm

27(28.5,30,31,32,34)cm

36(37,38,39.5,41,42.5)cm

FINSIHING:
Press as described on the
information page.
Join right shoulder seam.

Neckband
With RS facing, using 3mm needles and
yarn A, pick up and knit 16(16, 16, 18,
20, 20)sts down left side of front neck,
knit across 16(18, 18, 18, 26, 26)sts
from front neck holder, pick up and knit
16(16, 16, 18, 20, 20)sts up right side of
front neck, 2sts down right side of back
neck, knit across 32(34, 34, 34, 42, 42)sts
from back neck holder, and pick up and
knit 2sts up left side of back neck.
84[88, 88, 92, 112, 112]sts.

Work 4 rows in moss st patt.

Cast off in moss st patt.

Join left shoulder and neckband seams.

Sew in sleeves.

Join side and sleeve seams.

ABBReViATiONS

K – knit

P – purl

st(s) – stitch(es)

inc – increas(e)(ing)

dec – decreas(e)(ing)

st st – stocking stitch (1 row knit, 1 row purl)

g st – garter stitch (every row knit)

beg – begin(ning)

foll – following

rem – remain(ing)

alt – alternate

cont – continue

patt – pattern

tog – together

mm – millimetres

cm – centimetres

in – inch(es)

RS – right side

WS – wrong side

sl 1 – slip one stitch

psso – pass slipped stitch over

p2sso – pass 2 slipped stitches over

tbl – through back of loop

m1 – make one stitch by picking up loop between last and next stitch and working into the back of this loop

yfwd - bring yarn forward between the needles and then back over before making the next stitch. 1 st inc'd.

meas – measures

wyif – with yarn in front

wyib – with yarn at back

pm – place marker

ROWAN STOCKISTS

AUSTRALIA: Australian Country Spinners, Pty Ltd, Level 7, 409 St. Kilda Road, Melbourne Vic 3004.
Tel: 03 9380 3888   Fax: 03 9820 0989
Email: customerservice@auspinners.com.au

AUSTRIA: : MEZ Harlander GmbH, Schulhof 6, 1. Stock, 1010 Wien, Austria
Tel: + 00800 26 27 28 00   Fax: (00) 49 7644 802-133   Email: verkauf.
harlander@mezcrafts.com   Web: www.mezcrafts.at

BELGIUM: MEZ crafts Belgium NV, c/o MEZ GmbH, Kaiserstr. 1, 79341 Kenzingen Germany Tel: 0032 (0) 800 77 89 2
Fax: 00 49 7644 802 133   Email: sales.be-nl@mezcrafts.com
Web: www.mezcrafts.be

BULGARIA: MEZ Crafts Bulgaria EOOD, Bul. Rozhen 25A, BG-1220 Sofia,
Bulgaria Tel: +359 2 439 24 24   Fax: +359 2 439 24 28
Email: office.bg@mezcrafts.com

CHINA: Commercial agent Mr Victor Li, c/o MEZ GmbH Germany, Kaiserstr. 1, 79341 Kenzingen / Germany
Tel: (86- 21) 13816681825   Email: victor.li@mezcrafts.com

CHINA: SHANGHAI YUJUN CO., LTD., Room 701 Wangjiao Plaza, No.175 Yan'an(E), 200002 Shanghai, China
Tel: +86 2163739785   Email: jessechang@vip.163.com

CYPRUS: MEZ Crafts Bulgaria EOOD, Bul. Rozhen 25A, BG-1220 Sofia,
Bulgaria Tel: +359 2 439 24 24   Fax: +359 2 439 24 28
Email: office.bg@mezcrafts.com

CZECH REPUBLIC: Coats Czecho s.r.o. Staré Mesto 246 569 32
Tel: (420) 461616633   Email: galanterie@coats.com

DENMARK: Carl J. Permin A/S Egegaardsvej 28 DK-2610 Rødovre
Tel: (45) 36 72 12 00 E-mail: permin@permin.dk

ESTONIA: MEZ Crafts Estonia OÜ, Ampri tee 9/4, 74001 Viimsi Harjumaa
Tel: +372 630 6252   Email: info.ee@mezcrafts.com
Web: www.coatscrafts.co.ee

FINLAND: MEZ Crafts Finland Oy, Huhtimontie 6, 04200 Kerava
Tel: (358) 9 274 871   Email: sales.fi@mezcrafts.com
www.coatscrafts.fi

FRANCE: 3bcom, 35 avenue de Larrieu, 31094 Toulouse cedex 01, France
Tel: 0033 (0) 562 202 096   Email: Commercial@3b-com.com

GERMANY: MEZ GmbH, Kaiserstr. 1, 79341 Kenzingen, Germany
Tel: 0049 7644 802 222   Email: kenzingen.vertrieb@mezcrafts.com   Fax: 0049 7644 802 300
Web: www.mezcrafts.de

GREECE: MEZ Crafts Bulgaria EOOD, Bul. Rozhen 25A, BG-1220 Sofia,
Bulgaria Tel: +359 2 439 24 24   Fax: +359 2 439 24 28   Email: office.bg@mezcrafts.com

HOLLAND: G. Brouwer & Zn B.V., Oudhuijzerweg 69, 3648 AB Wilnis,
Netherlands Tel: 0031 (0) 297-281 557
Email: info@gbrouwer.nl

HONG KONG: East Unity Company Ltd, Unit B2, 7/F., Block B, Kailey Industrial Centre, 12 Fung Yip Street, Chai Wan
Tel: (852)2869 7110   Email: eastunityco@yahoo.com.hk

ICELAND: Carl J. Permin A/S Egegaardsvej 28 DK-2610 Rødovre
Tel: (45) 36 72 12 00 Email: permin@permin.dk

ITALY: Mez Cucirini Italy Srl, Viale Sarca, 223, 20126 MILANO
Tel.: 02 636151 Fax: 02 66111701

JAPAN: Hobbyra Hobbyre Corporation, 23-37, 5-Chome, Higashi-Ohi, Shinagawa-Ku, 1400011 Tokyo. Tel +81334721104
Daidoh International, 3-8-11 Kudanminami Chiyodaku, Hiei Kudan Bldg 5F, 1018619 Tokyo. Tel +81-3-3222-7076   Fax +81-3-3222-7066

KOREA: My Knit Studio, 3F, 144 Gwanhun-Dong, 110-300 Jongno-Gu, Seoul
Tel: 82-2-722-0006   Email: myknit@myknit.com   Web: www.myknit.com

LATVIA: Coats Latvija SIA, Mukusalas str. 41 b, Riga LV-1004
Tel: +371 67 625173   Fax: +371 67 892758   Email: info.latvia@coats.com
Web: www.coatscrafts.lv

LEBANON: y.knot, Saifi Village, Mkhalissiya Street 162, Beirut
Tel: (961) 1 992211   Fax: (961) 1 315553   Email: y.knot@cyberia.net.lb

LITHUANIA & RUSSIA: MEZ Crafts Lithuania UAB,A. Juozapaviciaus str. 6/2,
LT-09310 Vilnius Tel: +370 527 30971   Fax: +370 527 2305   Email: info.lt@mezcrafts.com   Web: www.coatscrafts.lt

LUXEMBOURG: Coats N.V., c/o Coats GmbH, Kaiserstr. 1, 79341 Kenzingen, Germany Tel: 00 49 7644 802 222   Fax: 00 49 7644 802 133
Email: sales.coatsninove@coats.com Web: www.coatscrafts.be

MEXICO: Estambres Crochet SA de CV, Aaron Saenz 1891-7Pte, 64650 MONTERREY TEL +52 (81) 8335-3870
Email: abremer@redmundial.com.mx

NEW ZEALAND: ACS New Zealand, P.O Box 76199, Northwood, Christchurch, New Zealand Tel: 64 3 323 6665   Fax: 64 3 323 6660
Email: lynn@impactmg.co.nz

NORWAY: Carl J. Permin A/S Egegaardsvej 28 DK-2610 Rødovre
Tel: (45) 36 72 12 00   E-mail: permin@permin.dk

PORTUGAL: Mez Crafts Portugal, Lda – Av.Vasco da Gama, 774 - 4431-059 V.N,
Gaia, Portugal Tel: 00 351 223 770700 Email: sales.iberia@mezcrafts.com

SINGAPORE: Golden Dragon Store, BLK 203 Henderson Rd #07-02, 159546 Henderson Indurstrial Park Singapore
Tel: (65) 62753517   Fax: (65) 62767112   Email: gdscraft@hotmail.com

SLOVAKIA: MEZ Crafts Slovakia, s.r.o. Seberíniho 1, 821 03 Bratislava,
Slovakia Tel: +421 2 32 30 31 19   Email: galanteria@mezcrafts.com

SOUTH AFRICA: Arthur Bales LTD, 62 4th Avenue, Linden 2195
Tel: (27) 11 888 2401 Fax: (27) 11 782 6137   Email: arthurb@new.co.za
Web: www.arthurbales.co.za

SPAIN: MEZ Fabra Spain S.A, Avda Meridiana 350, pta 13 D, 08027 Barcelona Tel: +34 932908400   Fax: +34 932908409 Email: atencion.clientes@mezcrafts.com

SWEDEN: Carl J. Permin A/S Egegaardsvej 28 DK-2610 Rødovre
Tel: (45) 36 72 12 00 E-mail: permin@permin.dk

SWITZERLAND: MEZ Crafts Switzerland GmbH, Stroppelstrasse20, 5417 Untersiggenthal, Switzerland Tel: +41 00800 2627 2800   Fax: 0049 7644 802 133   Web: www.mezcrafts.ch

TURKEY: MEZ Crafts Tekstil A.□, Kavacık Mahallesi, Ekinciler Cad. Necip Fazıl Sok. No.8 Kat: 5, 34810 Beykoz / Istanbul
Tel: +90 216 425 88 10   www.mezcrafts.com

TAIWAN: Cactus Quality Co Ltd, 7FL-2, No. 140, Sec.2 Roosevelt Rd, Taipei, 10084 Taiwan, R.O.C. Tel: 00886-2-23656527   Fax: 886-2-23656503
Email: cqcl@ms17.hinet.net

THAILAND: Global Wide Trading, 10 Lad Prao Soi 88, Bangkok 10310
Tel: 00 662 933 9019   Fax: 00 662 933 9110
Email: global.wide@yahoo.com

U.K: Mez Craft UK Ltd, 17F Brooke's Mill, Armitage Bridge Huddersfield, HD4 7NR   Tel: +44 (0) 1484 768878   Fax: +44 (0) 1484 690 838
Web: www.knitrowan.com

INFORMATION

TENSION
This is the size of your knitting. Most of the knitting patterns will have a tension quoted. This is how many stitches 10cm/4in in width and how many rows 10cm/4in in length to make a square. If your knitting doesn't match this then your finished garment will not measure the correct size. To obtain the correct measurements for your garment you must achieve the tension.

The tension quoted on a ball band is the manufacturer's average. For the manufacturer and designers to produce designs they have to use a tension for you to be able to obtain the measurements quoted. It's fine not to be the average, but you need to know if you meet the average or not. Then you can make the necessary adjustments to obtain the correct measurements.

CHOOSING YARN
Choosing yarn, as one of my friends once described "It is like shopping in an adult's sweetie shop". I think this sums it up very well. All the colours and textures, where do you start? Look for the thickness, how chunky do you want your finished garment? Sometimes it's colour that draws you to a yarn or perhaps you have a pattern that requires a specific yarn. Check the washing/care instructions before you buy.

Yarn varies in thickness; there are various descriptions such as DK and 4ply these are examples of standard weights. There are a lot of yarns available that are not standard and it helps to read the ball band to see what the recommended needle size is.

This will give you an idea of the approximate thickness. It is best to use the yarn recommended in the pattern.

Keep one ball band from each project so that you have a record of what you have used and most importantly how to care for your garment after it has been completed. Always remember to give the ball band with the garment if it is a gift.

The ball band normally provides you with the average tension and recommended needle sizes for the yarn, this may vary from what has been used in the pattern, always go with the pattern as the designer may change needles to obtain a certain look. The ball band also tells you the name of the yarn and what it is made of, the weight and approximate length of the ball of yarn along with the shade and dye lot numbers. This is important as dye lots can vary, you need to buy your yarn with matching dye lots.

PRESSING AND AFTERCARE
Having spent so long knitting your project it can be a great shame not to look after it properly. Some yarns are suitable for pressing once you have finished to improve the look of the fabric. To find out this information you will need to look on the yarn ball band, where there will be washing and care symbols.

Once you have checked to see if your yarn is suitable to be pressed and the knitting is a smooth texture (stocking stitch for example), pin out and place a damp cloth onto the knitted pieces. Hold the steam iron (at the correct temperature) approximately 10cm/4in away from the fabric and steam. Keep the knitted pieces pinned in place until cool.

As a test it is a good idea to wash your tension square in the way you would expect to wash your garment.

WITH THANKS

q u a i l s t u d i o would like to thank Tom Leighton
for his amazing photography, and our design team
for their work on this project. To our dedicated team
of knitters who work so hard to bring our designs to
life. Our models Indiana and Austin along with their
parents for their superb modelling and assistance.
Also to the Royal National Rose Society for allowing us
the use of their location for photography. Then finally
David and the team at Rowan for their support on this
project and yarn sponsorship.